Original title:
Golden Hour on the Beach

Copyright © 2025 Creative Arts Management OÜ
All rights reserved.

Author: Ronan Whitfield
ISBN HARDBACK: 978-1-80581-546-4
ISBN PAPERBACK: 978-1-80581-073-5
ISBN EBOOK: 978-1-80581-546-4

A Glisten on the Water's Edge

Sunburnt toes in the sand,
Flipping burgers with one hand.
Seagulls plotting on a quest,
Stealing fries, they're quite the pest.

Kids splash water like it's gold,
A dolphin jumps and makes me bold.
We laugh as tides bring in the sea,
Who knew wet socks would make us free?

The Duskwalker's Path

Footprints dance on twilight's stage,
Crabs applauding with no rage.
A surfboard race against the breeze,
Mismatched flip-flops, oh what a tease!

Friends play tag with sandcastles,
While dad falls trying to wrassles.
The sunset sparkles, not a care,
Just watch the wind mess up my hair!

Fading Echoes of Brightness

The beach ball's squeak makes us laugh,
As tides erase our goofy craft.
A wave crashes, sending us high,
Like little boats we bob and fly.

With ice cream cones that melt away,
We cheer for the end of the day.
Sunset hues all mix and swirl,
As I chase my runaway girl.

Scrolls of Light Above the Deep

The sun scribbles on the sea,
Doodles dancing, wild and free.
We share jokes that cause a roar,
As waves wash up at the shore.

Toward the horizon, laughter spreads,
Like kites caught in sunbeam threads.
The ocean smiles, a cheeky grin,
As we plan to dive right back in.

Whispering Tides at Dusk

The seagulls squawking, what a sight,
They dive for snacks just out of flight.
Sunset drapes the sand in gold,
While beach balls bounce, oh so bold.

Sandcastles crumble, it's a race,
With moats and towers, just a trace.
Little feet run, laughter rings,
Who knew the coast held such silly things?

Celestial Fire Above Waves

The sky ignites, a playful show,
As flip-flops fly, and kids all go.
A crusty crab is quite the clown,
He pinches toes, then scuttles down.

With ice cream drips and sticky hands,
We join the dance, like marching bands.
The ocean giggles, waves do leap,
As we lose track of time, and sleep.

Sunset Serenade

A ukulele strums a tune so sweet,
As kids chase shadows on bare feet.
A sunset wave, a splash so grand,
With laughter ringing across the land.

As twilight whispers, stories unfold,
Of jellyfish tales and pirates bold.
A sudden wave and squeals abound,
Who knew such joy could be so found?

Coral Skies and Silken Sands

The clouds are painted with a wink,
While beach towels roll, and drinks do clink.
Sandy toes dance to the ocean's sway,
In this whimsical, fun-filled play.

With shades askew and hats askance,
We prance and twirl, oh what a chance!
The sunset smiles, the day's a blast,
Forever holds this moment fast.

Whispers of the Dying Day

The sun shrinks low, a golden fling,
Seagulls squawk, oh what a zing!
Kids run wild, they take a dive,
Splashing water, they laugh, they thrive.

A beach ball flies, a dog takes aim,
Chasing shadows, it's all a game.
Sunscreen slips, oh what a sight,
Furry friends in a brawl tonight.

Velvet Tides at Sunset

Waves lap softly at the shore,
Tickling toes, like a playful chore.
The sand, a blanket for our feet,
Laughter echoing, oh so sweet.

A crab scuttles, quick in flight,
Hermit homes look quite a fright.
Ice cream melts, it drips and runs,
Sticky fingers, oh what fun!

Glowing Memories in the Twilight

The sky's a canvas, painted bright,
We giggle as we catch a kite.
Flip-flops flying, someone trips,
What a show, a dance of slips!

A picnic spread, sandwiches askew,
Seagulls eyeing what's left of stew.
Laughter bursts like soda pop,
The fun won't end, it's non-stop!

Sunlit Sands and Whispering Winds

The breeze whispers secrets, oh so sly,
While sunscreen stings, we break a sigh.
Umbrellas tilt, a tumbledown mess,
Our beachwear's a mismatched dress!

Tanned folks volley with a splash,
Belly flops make quite a crash.
Seashells glisten, treasures we find,
While crabs plot, ever so unkind.

Where Horizons Embrace the Sun

Seagulls squawk with great delight,
As beachgoers sprint, avoiding the bite.
Flip-flops fly and sunscreen spills,
While laughter echoes over the hills.

Children dig for treasure with glee,
Building castles, oh so fancy-free.
A wave crashes, plans swept away,
As sand becomes a playful buffet.

Serenity in the Dimming Glow

The sun dips low, a painted sky,
While hot dogs roast, birds idly fly.
Towel soccer turns into a slip,
As someone takes an accidental dip.

Napping, I dream, with sunburned cheeks,
And sunscreen residue that squeaks.
Near the shoreline, a crab ambushes,
In my flip-flops, it cunningly crushes.

Chasing Shadows at Twilight's Edge

Shadows grow long, we dance and prance,
Playing tag with a goofy stance.
A beach ball flies with woeful grace,
Headed straight for a stranger's face.

Laughter erupts, the waves agree,
As ice cream drips down knee to knee.
Sun-hats twirl like dancing hats,
While sandcastles stand against all stats.

A Tapestry of Colors Unfolds

Hues of orange, pink, and yellow,
Skimpy swimsuits, oh so mellow.
I trip on a towel, I trip again,
As my friends mock me, like it's a game.

Kites are caught in a gusty gust,
Flying high, or in the dust.
A dog steals my sandwich, oh what luck,
And my beach hat? Well, it's now stuck.

Dappled Light on Ocean's Edge

The sun hangs low, a giant fry,
Seagulls squawk as they pass by.
Kids chase waves in silly glee,
While crabs plot their escape, oh me!

Buckets tipped, and sandcastles fall,
A wet dog runs with laughter's call.
Flip-flops flying, a race to the sea,
Splashing friends like it's all for free.

Beachballs bounce and sunscreens fly,
The perfect day, oh my, oh my!
Corny jokes and laughter's song,
As sunlight hums where we belong.

The Evening's Gentle Breath

Waves whisper jokes to the shore,
As surfers fall and swim once more.
Flip-flops squeak on heated sand,
As laughter dances, hand in hand.

Shadows stretch like sleepy cats,
Sandcastles conquered by cheeky chats.
A frisbee flies over giggles galore,
And seaside snacks we can't ignore.

A sunburned nose and puns to share,
Sandy hair and salty air.
The tide rolls in with a playful creep,
While we nestle down for laughter's leap.

Warmth of the Setting Sun

Sunset paints the world too bright,
As ice cream dribbles, what a sight!
A toddler giggles, slips, and falls,
Launching sand into distant calls.

Beach towels claim their rightful throne,
While parents nap, their phones have grown.
Kids dig deep, seek treasure near,
With wild hopes of finding a beer.

A seagull swoops, a daring dive,
Now, who's ready for the 'high-five'?
The ocean's laughter swells the fun,
Who knew the beach could weigh a ton?

Radiance Upon the Shore

Oh, the sun is blushing bright,
As we chase shadows, full of light.
Sandy toes and water fights,
Every splish, a pure delight.

Tanning butter on a nose,
A family feud with garden hose.
Umbrellas sail, a quirky scene,
While seagulls dive for snacks unseen.

Sunset glimmers, time to unwind,
A treasure map we've all designed.
Frolicking under citrus skies,
With salty snacks and silly ties.

Embracing the Dimming Sky

As the sun does pirouette, so bold,
The surf's turning chilly, drink's gone cold.
Seagulls squawk, plotting their next snack,
While I dance awkwardly, feeling a crack.

With each wave that crashes, my worries flee,
But tripping on sand is my specialty.
Flip-flops flying, oh what a sight,
In this fleeting light, I just might take flight!

Reflections of a Fiery End

The sun, a flamboyant orange ball,
Gives car alarms at dusk their call.
I ponder life's mysteries, sip my brew,
Why do my chips always fall in two?

Friends are laughing, making a scene,
As I attempt to show off my cuisine.
But the wind has plans, oh look at that!
My sandwich is sailing—who knew it could chat?

Shades of Gold Beneath the Clouds

Clouds wear their gold like a fancy dress,
While I struggle to find my focus, I guess.
My sunscreen's misplaced, oh what a plight,
Now I'm a lobster by dimming light!

Children are running, dodging the tide,
While I'm stuck here with my awkward pride.
Should I frolic or sit? Decisions, decisions!
Perhaps I'll just nap, avoid all collisions!

Serene Beauty of Sunset

The sky is an artist with colors bright,
My camera clicks—oops, wrong angle, right?
Friends laugh as I capture the sea,
But miss the shore, now that's just me!

The tide rolls in, and so do my fears,
What if I trip, fall, and plunge to my tears?
Instead, I jest, pretend to dive,
As my towel shouts, 'Look, you're alive!'

Tides Singing in Last Light

The waves wear their best, a sloshy suit,
Seagulls are dancing, in a feathered dispute.
Crabs throw a party, they scuttle and sway,
While sunbeams giggle, at the end of the day.

Sandcastles wobble, their towers may fall,
As kids chase each other, in a sandy free-for-all.
Buckets are tipping, splashes all around,
Laughter's the soundtrack, a joy-bubbling sound.

Beach balls are bouncing, a carnival show,
The sun wears a grin, as it starts to bow low.
Flip-flops are flying, a fashionable race,
With each twist and turn, they find their own place.

Just as the light winks, the day's brief encore,
Surfers ride jokes on the ocean's soft roar.
As shadows grow longer, and day bids goodbye,
The tides keep on singing, beneath the bright sky.

Where Dunes Meet Dimming Skies

Dunes sport their shadows, an odd kind of chap,
As kids dig for treasures, with squeals in their yap.
Kites in the air look like fish out of line,
While the sun's glowing cheeks turn a blush so fine.

Sandwiches vanish, a tasty delight,
And seagulls are plotting, a takeoff in flight.
A cooler's adventure, with soda that fizz,
While sunscreen's the champion, of number one whiz.

The horizon is laughing, with pinks and with gold,
As tales of the beach turn charmingly bold.
Footprints behind them, a trail of pure fun,
With giggles and splashes, they've danced till they're done.

As twilight approaches, with a wink from the tide,
The beach holds a secret, where memories abide.
Hearts filled with joy, and the sun's cheeky flare,
Where laughter's a melody, riding warm ocean air.

Elysian Glow Over Crystal Waters

The sun shows its teeth, a grin wide and bright,
As flip-flops go missing, in a daring flight.
Shells are on the hunt, for a treasure to show,
And sunhats are flipping, like stars in a show.

Waves splash a tune, with a bubbly refrain,
While kids leap in glee, on the soft, sandy plain.
Picnics in progress, with snacks on parade,
A feast of cold treats, in a sun-kissed cascade.

Like jelly, the sunset, wobbles on cue,
As laughter erupts, like the ocean's own brew.
Time's taking pictures, in shades deep and bold,
With giggles wrapped up in the soft, fading gold.

As day signs its lease, and the dusk takes a bow,
The beach stays a playground, with a cheeky vow.
So let's close our eyes, and laugh down the lane,
For memories made here, are joy's sweetest gain.

The Sun's Farewell Glow

The sun slips down, a cheeky prank,
Waves giggle softly, what a prank!
Seagulls swoop with a squawking tease,
Tiptoeing through the sand with ease.

Flip-flops fling off in a joy-filled shot,
Sandy toes wriggle, why not? Why not?
Crabs wear shades, who would have guessed?
Building castles, they're the best-dressed!

A beach ball zooms, an aerial flight,
Someone's sun hat takes off in fright.
Laughter erupts, as a splash goes wide,
In this sandy circus, we take a ride.

As twilight winks, the fun won't end,
The sky blushes pink like a cheeky friend.
With snacks and jokes, we roast as we toast,
This beachside fiesta, we love the most!

When Day Meets Night

The sun and moon dance a silly jig,
As if they're lost in a playful gig.
Stars start to twinkle, the stage is set,
For a beach bonanza we won't forget.

Towel fights break out, oh what a sight,
As shadows stretch long, bathing in light.
Sandcastles topple, with a goofy sigh,
While laughter and snacks bloom under the sky.

A frisbee flies, but heads dive down,
Curious seagulls wear a headless crown.
The ocean hums silly tunes on repeat,
As night falls softly on sandy feet.

With drinks in hand, we cheer the day's end,
And toast to the laughter, our faithful friend.
Under the stars, we dance and we play,
In this sparkly twilight, we want to stay!

Echoes of Twilight Shores

Waves whisper secrets, with wink and flap,
As if they're telling tales of a friendly mishap.
Footprints sketch stories in the golden grain,
While surfboards wait for a new joke to gain.

A lone flamingo struts, with swag galore,
Making grand moves like a beach dance floor.
Coolers fizz and splutter like soda pop dreams,
As laughter erupts in bubbly streams.

Picnic spreads out, a buffet of fun,
Sandwiches dance as we bask in the sun.
A friendly dog wanders with grace and style,
Stealing snacks and hearts all the while.

As day bids adieu, it winks with glee,
The tide rolls in with a fonder decree.
With each wave, we laugh, we glide, we soar,
In this sunset glow, we dance some more!

The Gilded Horizon

The horizon glitters, a golden smirk,
As waves crash on, all the waterwork.
A sandcastle team, united in cheer,
With seaweed crowns, it's a royal affair!

Beach games gathered like seagulls at play,
Frisbees and shells in a joyful ballet.
Someone slips, a slippery slide,
Laughter erupts, not a soul can hide.

Drinks in hand, with umbrellas bright,
We toast to the sunset, oh what a sight!
With stories weaving like shells in the sand,
In this whimsical world, we take a stand.

As the last light dims, jokes start to flow,
We celebrate moments, with hearts all aglow.
In the fading warmth, we find our bliss,
This shoreline magic, we won't dismiss!

Sunset's Blessing on the Shore

The sun slips down in a big orange slide,
As seagulls squawk and children collide.
There's ice cream drips and laughter galore,
While sandcastles tumble, who could ask for more?

We race past the waves, oh what a delight,
Except when my pants catch a rogue, salty bite.
With each awkward splash, my dignity flees,
As I try to swim like a duck with no knees.

Illuminated Serenity

The sky's dressed in pink, it's a colorful blend,
As my friend slips and falls, it's a comedy trend.
A rogue beach ball hits a poor fellow's face,
While others just giggle, adding to the grace.

Sand in my shorts, yes, I wear it with pride,
As a wave takes my drink, oh, what a ride!
The sun bids adieu, but we're not quite done,
We'll chase those last rays, oh this is such fun!

Sunset's Embrace

The sun waves goodbye in a dance so grand,
While I try to juggle my snacks in one hand.
A flip-flop flies off, oh what a disgrace,
I hop on one foot—would you laugh at my pace?

The beach blankets spread, like wild jellyfish,
While my brother attempts a heroic back-swish.
He lands in the surf, and oh how we roar,
His face full of seaweed, who could want more?

Waves of Amber Light

The sun's golden rays turn the surf into gold,
Kids scream and run, while the dog's feeling bold.
He chases his tail in a whirl of confusion,
As I can't stop laughing at this strange intrusion.

Ice cream cones melt like they're in a race,
As I get covered with whipped cream on my face.
We pose for a picture, but all I can see,
Is my dad's goofy grin—what a sight to be!

Nature's Lullaby at Day's Closure

The sun slips down, a golden nugget,
As seagulls squawk and steal my bucket.
The sand is warm, a cozy bed,
While crabs dance past, with sideways tread.

Surfers wipe out with a splash and a thud,
Eating granola, I watch them in mud.
A flip-flop flies, a weave of defeat,
Or was that just my lunch on repeat?

Children giggle, making sand pets,
A giant mound of dubious bets.
Their castles are topped with shells, oh so grand,
But watch out, here comes the tide's sneaky hand!

As dusk edges in, the laughter won't fade,
With shadows that lengthen, a billowed parade.
Nature's a joker, so full of surprise,
In this fading show, calm chaos will rise.

The Symphonic Dance of Sea and Sky

The sea hums softly, a lull of delight,
While clouds stomp about, quite ready to fight.
A kite in the air, a wild game of chase,
With each gusty laugh, it scrambles in space.

Lifesavers floating, their bright colors flash,
While beach balls bounce and go with a splash.
A crab tiptoes by, with a swagger to boast,
As waves giggle gently, they're ready to toast.

Oh look, there's a toddler, a cupcake in hand,
Critters unite for an edible band.
As seagulls debate who's stealing the fries,
The sunset is painted in pastel goodbyes.

The symphony ends, as jests take their leave,
Nature's humor only we'd believe.
With rustling laughter, the night takes its place,
Seashells will whisper, with a chuckle and grace.

Waves Clothed in Silence and Gold

The waves whisper secrets nobody hears,
While children throw sand, it's all cheers.
A dolphin pops up, in a playful jest,
As beachgoers cheer, "Hey, you do your best!"

Flip-flops are flung, a game of fetching,
As laughter erupts, and joy is stretching.
Barefoot romances, folly laid bare,
Who knew that true love would start with a pair?

Sunsets are canvas, painted with glee,
Starlit laughter drips down from the sea.
The towel is draped, in bright, silly pride,
And everybody dances, with sand at their side.

As the colors fade, a wink from the sky,
Nature nods softly, no need for a why.
In the twilight's light, we gather, we jest,
With waves clothed in warmth, we simply feel blessed.

A Radiant Farewell

The sun takes its bow, an encore of rays,
While beach bums collect all the shells from their plays.
A slapstick tumble, as someone trips near,
With a surfboard that holds all their snacks, I hear!

Coolers are spilling, drinks fly through the air,
A dog dashes past, without a single care.
It's a party on sands, from dusk until dark,
With friendships that sparkle like a bright playful lark.

As the shadows stretch long, the laughter ignites,
With flickering fireflies that join in the fights.
In this whimsical place, misunderstanding's the rule,
Who knew a sunburn could be such a jewel?

So here's to the day, where fun is the fare,
And each salty breeze carries a chuckle to share.
Under the blanket of twilight, let's smile and tell,
About waves and bright sunsets—a radiant farewell.

A Celestial Canvas

Sky painted orange, a splash of grace,
Seagulls dance wildly, a comical race.
Sandy toes giggle, a tickling game,
While sunscreen battles, a slippery fame.

Frolicking children, glittering sand,
Crabs with their antics, they just won't stand.
Umbrellas like mushrooms, a colorful sight,
Old men in speedos, oh what a fright!

Laughter erupts as a wave races in,
Splashing the tourists—oh, what a win!
A beach ball flies high, like it's on a quest,
But lands on a sunbather, oh, what a jest!

As shadows stretch long, the sun waves goodbye,
The day turns to memories that fly in the sky.

Blushing Skies and Teasing Waves

The sun winks low, a mischievous spark,
While toddlers chase seagulls, oh what a lark!
Flip-flops a-flying, they sprint with delight,
Face-plants in sand, what a hilarious sight!

Tanning attempts go hilariously wrong,
One burns like a lobster, can't take it long.
Picnics a-shamble, sandwiches flee,
While gulls steal the chips; oh, how they agree!

A paddleboarder tumbles, causally strolls,
Alligators in water? Just floating, oh no!
The beach is a stage; the fun never stops,
With laughter refracting off beachy backdrop.

As colors blend bright, day kisses night,
Smiles linger sweet, all feels so right.

Whispering Breeze at Dusk

A soft breeze hustles, tickling my ear,
With shadows that stretch, the laugh casts near.
Kites tangled high, like a dance gone awry,
Hats blown away, oh! There goes my supply!

Beach towels scatter as sand starts to creep,
Children march forth like a troop from deep sleep.
Buckets and shovels become castles and forts,
But only to find they attract the weird sorts!

As waves kick up splashes, they join in the chaos,
Bubbles in kids' laughter—an echoing pathos.
A chase for the frisbee, it flies like a dream,
Until a rogue wave snatches it, or so it seems!

Starlight creeps in, giggles float above,
Memories linger, and we dance like we love.

Fragments of Day in a Twilight Frame

Sunset arrives, like a silly parade,
Shades of purple, the laughter won't fade.
BBQ smoke mingles with sweet ocean air,
Friends try to juggle, but who really cares?

The beach ball bursts, chaos spreads wide,
As dogs chase their tails with cheeky pride.
Sandy snacks resemble a mix of delight,
While boisterous waves shine with silly light.

Old timers reminisce, tales filled with jest,
Each memory formed, like a game we all guessed.
As shadows grow long, and stars take their throne,
The whispers of fun become each rolling stone.

With laughter and joy, the night starts to bloom,
Good friends gathered, who needs more room?

Gleam of the Dying Day

On the shore where seagulls squawk,
Sandcastles lean like a wobbly clock.
Kids run wild, with shovels and grins,
While parents sip drinks, ignoring their sins.

Laughter erupts like waves at play,
A beach ball bounces—then flies away.
Flip-flops flop as they dash for the sea,
Time for a swim? Oh wait, not me!

Crabs scuttle sideways, a funny parade,
In this sandy kingdom where sunlight's made.
The sun dips low, it paints us in cheer,
And all of our worries just disappear!

As shadows grow long, the fun doesn't fade,
With tied-up hair and a wild charade.
With sand on our backs, we giggle and sway,
Under the sky, we'll never decay!

Fluid Gold of Fading Light

Shadows stretch out like a friendly ghost,
Sunscreen's a must, we slather and boast.
The Frisbee flies, it's a wicked throw,
Knocking down hats and dignity, oh no!

Children chase tides with squeals of delight,
While dads in their coolers contemplate flight.
A seagull steals chips right from the hand,
What a thief in this twilight land!

The umbrellas dance in the teasing breeze,
Some folks complain about sand on their knees.
But who cares, when the sun's in the sky?
We'll laugh and make waves until we're dry!

As day gives way to playful dusk tunes,
We gather our things, singing old cartoons.
The fluid light warms our silly hearts,
Forever beach tales, where laughter starts!

Waves Reverberating in Amber

The sun is a pancake, golden and round,
Bouncing off waves, where laughter is found.
Pail and shovel, a battle ensues,
Who can build castles without losing shoes?

Flipping for fish, a slip, and a splash,
An octopus cameo, a slippery clash.
Tides sweep in giggles, we dodge and we dive,
In this amber glow, we truly come alive!

Seashells are treasures, or so we declare,
A crab on the sand says, "Hey, I'm not scared!"
With wisecracks and puns, the jokes hit the shore,
As the sky blushes pink, we giggle for more.

As the sun nods goodnight, we wave with a grin,
Grains of the beach, caught under our skin.
Memories linger, and sand joins the fray,
Oh, to be silly, in the light of the day!

Serenity in the Dusk Glow

The beach turns to magic, with colors that whirl,
As parents dig deep in their cooler's pearl.
Kids chase the tide, they yell, "Look at me!"
While sand clings like glitter on noses with glee.

The sun's taking bows, a curtain of gold,
While laughter and stories begin to unfold.
A dog steals a sandwich, then runs with delight,
As the ocean plays music, softening the night.

With flip-flops a-flop, we dance in the sand,
Armloads of shells slip right from our hand.
The breeze is a jester, playful and spry,
As we watch seabirds dive and hear gulls fly by.

The flicker of twilight steals hearts with a grin,
As the day fades away, we just can't help but spin.
In every wave's whisper, and twilight's soft glow,
We find joy and laughter, oh how we love the show!

Beyond the Horizon's Glow

The sun dips low, it's quite a show,
Seagulls squawk, and crabs do their stroll.
I trip on sand, a funny twist,
And laugh with waves, I can't resist.

Friends bring snacks, like chips in hand,
A race for fries, we make our stand.
But mid the fun, a seagull swoops,
And steals a fry from all our groups.

With shades askew, we chase the bird,
It cackles loud, that cheeky nerd.
Our laughter rings as it takes flight,
We trip again, it's pure delight.

As sunbeams dance in colors bright,
We build our castles, oh what a sight!
And in our hearts, this joy we save,
While salty winds give us a wave.

A Dance of Light and Shadow

Shadows stretch as the sun goes down,
We trip and fall, it's quite a clown.
Footprints race in a zig-zag way,
As laughter echoes through the bay.

A frisbee flies, but not so high,
It lands on my head; oh my, oh my!
With each laugh, the dolphins leap,
We dance with waves, and secrets keep.

An old dog snoozes, dreaming wide,
While kids make sandcastles with pride.
But watch out! A rogue wave rushes in,
Turn and run, let the chaos begin!

The golden hue fades fast away,
Yet laughter heals as we play.
With sticky hands and sandy feet,
We run for ice cream, oh what a treat!

Tranquility Between Twilight

As twilight falls, the light turns dim,
We spot a crab, that little whim.
With tiny claws, it scurries quick,
A flash of humor, oh, what a trick!

The beach umbrellas bend and bow,
A playful dance, we all know how.
While sand between our toes does squeak,
We share old jokes that make us weak.

A flip-flop flies! Oh what a sight,
It lands right in the bonfire light.
As marshmallows roast, we chat and cheer,
And ponder why we came right here.

With starlit skies, the laughter swells,
We tell tall tales, weaving spells.
Through quirky moments, our spirits lift,
In golden gleams, we find our gift.

Reflections in the Melting Sun

The ball bounces, but flies away,
We sprint to catch it, what a day!
With sandy knees and sun-kissed cheeks,
We chuckle loud, oh how it peaks!

A kite above, it tangles fast,
We tug and pull, what a blast!
Then it dips low, we gasp in fright,
But up it goes, soaring in flight.

Our towels are sprawled, a patchwork glow,
In the mix, a snack or two we throw.
But ants invade our picnic feast,
And we all shout, "Hey! At least!"

As laughter floats on the evening breeze,
We wave goodbye to that sticky cheese.
In the fading light, we find our cheer,
With every giggle, we hold it dear.

Drifting on Sunbeams

Seagulls sing their silly song,
While sun rays dance, where we belong.
We try to pose, but then we fall,
On shifting sands, we sprawl and sprawl.

A beach ball rolls into a moody crab,
He pinches toes; oh what a jab!
We chase our hats, the wind's a tease,
Laughing loud with salty ease.

With sunscreen smeared on every nose,
We shine like stars in beachy prose.
As waves come crashing, oh so grand,
We splash and giggle, hand in hand.

And just before the sun departs,
We build a tower with silly parts.
It leans and wobbles, about to crash,
Another day ends with a splash.

Sandcastles in the Glimmering Light

Buckets clank, it's building time,
We sculpt with joy and lots of grime.
A castle grand, or maybe not,
The walls collapse; oh, what a plot!

We add a moat, with seaweed flair,
Our masterpiece is beyond compare.
But here comes tide, with a sneaky creep,
Our sandy fort falls into sleep.

A crab decides it's quite a throne,
Sits on the tower we call our own.
We laugh and watch our dreams go splat,
Who needs a castle? We have a mat!

When the sun dips low, we shed a tear,
To say goodbye, our joy sincere.
"Next time," we vow, "we'll make it last!"
But really, who can build that fast?

The Dappled Glow of Ocean's Breath

Footprints scattered on the shore,
We chase the waves and then explore.
The tide pulls back with funny quirks,
As slippery sand makes clumsy jerks.

A leap and splash, we're soaked anew,
We giggle at the ocean's view.
A beach ball flies, then lands with grace,
Right on a sunbather's funny face!

We spot a jellyfish, wobbly and round,
It dances lightly without a sound.
We ponder if it's jelly or jam,
But plunge right back; we don't give a damn!

Under the sun, we laugh and play,
With tiny treasures from the bay.
As colors swirl in evening's hue,
We know tomorrow holds more mischief too!

Reflections at Day's End

The sky ignites in tangerine,
While we race 'round in a playful scene.
A kite goes up, then upside down,
As laughter ripples all over town.

We try to take a perfect pic,
But someone trips—a real slapstick!
With squirting water and jumping glee,
This funny dance is pure esprit.

The shoreline glows with golden rays,
We strike a pose—then quickly sway!
A seagull swoops for chips galore,
And we just can't help but want more!

As shadows stretch and night descends,
We gather round, our day transcends.
With salty cheeks and sun-kissed skin,
We'll be back for another spin!

Serenity Between the Shores

Seagulls squawk, what a blast,
Chasing each other, oh so fast.
Sandy toes and laughter swell,
As crabs plot their own beachy hell.

Sandcastles rise, then they fall,
Oops, a wave took one, what a brawl!
Ice cream drips, a sticky treat,
Who knew seagulls could be so fleet?

Bikini tops and sunburned skin,
To sit or swim? Where to begin?
Beach volleyball, a hit or miss,
A ball to the face, oh what bliss!

As the tide rolls in with a tease,
We laugh so hard, we drop to our knees.
The sunset paints, a wild hue,
We wave goodbye, to this crazy view.

Warm Embraces of Day's End

Coconut water, a tropical fling,
The beach is alive, can you hear it sing?
Flip-flops flying, oh what a sight,
A race to the shore, who will win the fight?

Sunscreen battles, slippery foes,
Missed a spot, now it glows.
Beach towels flapping, all over the sand,
Like flags of fun, across this land.

A beach ball bounces from here to there,
Someone scores, but do they care?
Sand in sandwiches, a crunchy bite,
The joy of this mess, pure delight!

As laughter ebbs with the outgoing tide,
We gather our treasures, hearts open wide.
The sun dips low, a final cheer,
To this silly day, we raise a beer!

Caress of the Waning Day

Waves whisper secrets in salty tones,
While jellyfish dance, like forgotten drones.
A beach umbrella, flipping in glee,
It's a windy day, let's call it spree!

Tacos are served, sand on a plate,
Seagull steals one—what's its fate?
"Catch me if you can!" we all boast,
But alas, we just serve it as toast!

Bizarre wide-brim hats, look at those styles,
Worn with confidence, they bring on smiles.
A sand-encrusted selfie, what a jest,
Who needs glamour? This is the best!

The sun dips low, with a wink and a grin,
Back to the shack, let the fun begin.
We raise our drinks, as the crickets prance,
Here's to good times, let's boogie and dance!

The Light that Lingers

Crashing waves hide whispers of glee,
While sun hats hover like bees on a spree.
Belly flops echo, everyone shrieks,
Timing's an art, but who even peeks?

Footprints scatter like lost little dreams,
Chasing after kites, or so it seems.
Flip-flop flops, a woeful sound,
As someone stumbles—who's on the ground?

Potato sack races, the seaweed wraps,
Messy hairdos and terrible naps.
Ice cream cones melting under the sun,
Who knew beach days could be this fun?

With skies growing dim, we sit side by side,
Sharing these moments with warmth and pride.
The light that lingers, a hug of the night,
In this wacky world, everything's right!

Twilight's Warm Embrace

The sun gives a wink, what a flirt,
While flip-flops squawk where the sand's been hurt.
Seagulls steal fries, oh what a heist!
We laugh as they dive, like they're thinking twice.

Kids build castles, but they all fall down,
Splashing mud on dad, oh what a clown!
Mom rolls her eyes, then joins in the fun,
And soon all are drenched in a splashy run.

The beach ball deflates with a silly flop,
Like a snail on a mission, it'll never stop.
Someone shouts, "Watch out!" but it's too late now,
As the dog leaps high, and takes a bow.

With laughter echoing, the day drifts away,
As colors swirl, we frolic and sway.
The breeze tells stories, the night draws near,
As we chase distant fireflies, grinning ear to ear.

Radiance Between Tides

Bubbles pop loudly in a wild parade,
As sunscreen warriors display their trade.
With each slathered dollop, a battle is won,
Against tan lines willing to ruin the fun.

Waves crash and tumble, a slippery spree,
A jellyfish floats by, quite boldly, you see.
We skirt past the squish, with giggles and glee,
As a frisbee flies past, just missed a bee!

Sun hats fly off in the wind's cheeky grasp,
And laughter erupts as we blindly clasp.
Sandcastles teeter, not meant to survive,
But jokes fill the air — oh, this is the vibe!

As night starts to fall, with a wink and a tease,
We gather our treasures, soft breezed with ease.
With toast to the sunset, our hearts find their glow,
While stars peek out, putting on quite the show.

Echoes of Dusk and Dawn

A surfboard crashes, but wait, there's more!
Someone lands sideways, a bungled encore!
The ocean's a stage, with laughter the script,
As sunscreen soldiers slide, tightly zip-lipped.

An ice cream disaster, the cone starts to melt,
As sticky fingers plague where sweet tooth is felt.
We tumble and giggle in sugary delight,
While seagulls, with sneers, plan their next kite flight.

Sand stuck in hair, oh what a style!
With driftwood as props, we all strike a smile.
The sun waves goodbye with a wink in the sky,
While we dance to the rhythm of waves rolling by.

The moon takes its place, as the stars start to blink,
And we build sandy dreams with a thoughtful wink.
In this moment of joy, we feel so alive,
As we race towards tomorrow, with fun to revive!

Luminous Sands Beneath a Distant Sky

A crab high-fives a toddler with glee,
While seashells gossip, as friends like to be.
The sun wobbles, casting its golden delight,
On dreams of bright laughter, all poised for a flight.

A beach volleyball zooms through the air,
Landing straight on a big lady's hair.
With oohs and aahhs, we all burst in cheer,
As she spins around, a new style to wear!

The tide gently teases our toes in a game,
While dad does the worm, still chasing his fame.
A dance with the dolphins, yet none can compare,
To the joy of our hearts, the salt in our hair.

As twilight brushes the sand, we retreat,
With memories etched in our soles, what a treat!
The stars start to twinkle, with laughter in store,
As we dream of the beach adventures in lore.

Where Sunlight Meets the Sea

The sun's round belly starts to grin,
As waves dance in a cheeky spin.
Flip-flops fly like fish in flight,
While seagulls cackle, what a sight!

The children giggle, running wild,
Chasing crabs, each one a child.
Sandcastles stand proud, but oh dear,
A rogue wave comes and we all fear!

A beach ball bounces, caught in flight,
Hits a sunbather, what a fright!
"Hey, that's my drink!" she shouts in play,
As laughter echoes through the bay.

Sunsets hand out a carnival show,
With hues of orange and hints of glow.
The tide rolls in for a curtain call,
As night whispers softly: "Come one, come all!"

Luminous Sands at Sundown

The glow of day, it starts to fade,
Fishermen boast, "Look at our trade!"
With fish as big as dreams can be,
They trip on nets, too blind to see.

Picnic spreads on checkered cloths,
While ants march in, so brave, so oft!
A sandwich flies, a child's mishap,
As seagulls swoop and share a clap.

The volleyball bounces with joyous cheer,
"Not in my face!" we laugh, oh dear!
While beach folks argue about the tan,
"Who's more golden? Come take a scan!"

As twilight whispers secrets wide,
We stake our claims, we take our stride.
And twilight twirls, a playful sprite,
Chasing shadows into night's delight.

Pink Hues and Soft Shadows

A canvas spreads above the sea,
With shades of pineapple and zestful glee.
The sun bows low, a royal king,
While laughter fills the air, a spring!

Sandy toes tell tales of play,
As a crab scuttles and makes its way.
"Watch your step!" a voice does shout,
Another flip-flop's thrown about!

Tissue floats like boats on dreams,
In the waves that giggle and tease.
"Who's for ice cream?" a shout rings true,
As sprinkles fly, we yell, "Woohoo!"

As pink hues wrap the day with sighs,
We ponder life, with laughter and fries.
Little feet race to greet the breeze,
As evening falls, it's all a tease!

The Last Light's Caress

The sun dips low, a cheeky wink,
As jellyfish dance near the brink.
"A splash fight?" a daring shout,
And splatter soars, without a doubt!

With pails and shovels, dreams take flight,
As tides come in to join the fight.
"Who built that castle?" a voice does gleam,
But waves are plotting their own scheme.

The beach bonfire starts to glow,
S'mores appear in a gooey show.
But someone's won, they take the prize,
A marshmallow flung—oh my, surprise!

As laughter fades with the fading rays,
We gather round for fun-filled days.
The last light winks as night takes throne,
With tales to share when we get home.

Twilight's Painted Canvas

The sun waves goodbye with a cheeky grin,
Seagulls in sunglasses, they start to spin.
Footprints in sand, what a hilarious sight,
As a crab steals my sandwich, oh what a night!

Kids chase the waves, their shrieks fill the air,
Splashing each other, without a care.
A dog in a hat, he thinks he can surf,
But all he does is tumble, oh what a turf!

Colors collide, in a playful rush,
The sky turns to orange, then fades into blush.
With ice cream in hand, it drips on my toes,
Laughter erupts, as the sunset bestows.

We dance on the sand, our shadows in tow,
Twisting like jelly, just putting on a show.
As night begins falling, we shiver and squeak,
Who knew beach days could be so unique?

Sunbeams and Silhouettes

The sun dips low, with a wink and a tease,
Sunscreen's gone rogue, it's hard to believe!
Somebody's hat flies, like it's got a mind,
The wind giggles softly, leaving chaos behind.

Seashells are us, in a fashion parade,
The crabs are the judges, at this grand charade.
We prance under rays, like we own the whole show,
But trip and fall flat—now that's quite the blow!

Someone brought snacks, we gather to feast,
Until ants join the party, and then we're released.
The tide's rolling in, with a playful sock,
And we run from the water, laughing in shock!

As the horizon blinks, it's a quirky display,
The colors all clash, in a whimsical way.
In dusk's sweet embrace, we breathe out a sigh,
Just another sunset, and oh my, oh my!

Glistening Ripples of Gold

Waves dance like toddlers, carefree and wild,
A starfish is posing, oh look at that child!
With sunglasses on fish, what a curious sight,
They're plotting a party, with the moon's invite.

A breeze whispers secrets, to the tall swaying grass,
While seagulls tell tales of their day at the class.
Beach balls are flying, with giggles they soar,
Then land in my drink—oh, what a great score!

Kites swirl like dragons, in the pastel sky,
A dance-off ensues, while the waves bounce high.
Then someone drops sand, in an epic kitchen sink,
And we're laughing it off, with a cheeky wink!

As day turns to night, with a splash and a cheer,
We toast to the laughter, the memories near.
With a wink to the stars, our hearts light and bold,
We savor this moment, like glistening gold.

Shimmers of Dusk's Palette

The day takes a bow, with a comical twist,
Shadows of folks, doing the cha-cha just missed.
A gentle breeze whispers, tickling my skin,
And the dog steals a hot dog, oh where to begin?

Surfboards are lined up, like fish on a grill,
A flip of the hair, and the kids can't sit still.
What's chasing us now? It's just an old shoe!
But watch for that wave—it's coming for you!

With laughter, we gather, to watch the sky glow,
Soft purples and pinks, putting on a show.
But who brought the fireworks? And where's the display?

Turns out it's just dolphins, making their way!

As twilight arrives, we pack up and giggle,
With sandy-flecked faces, we jump and we wiggle.
A sunset so silly, it stole all our hearts,
Here's to beach days and all of their arts!

The Brushstrokes of Evening

The sun spills paint upon the shore,
Where seagulls laugh and children roar.
A crab in shades of pink and teal,
Waves goodbye with a crustacean squeal.

Flip-flops flying, oh what a sight,
Dancing patterns with sheer delight.
A beach ball strikes a wayward kite,
Both caught in a playful, swirling flight.

Buckets and spades in frantic chase,
Sandcastles crumble in quite the race.
"Watch out!" a voice shrieks from the back,
As a wave unleashes a splash attack!

With grins as broad as the horizon line,
Sunsets blend like mismatched wine.
Laughs echo as the day unwinds,
In hues where every whim aligns.

Glistening Trails of Ebbing Tides

Footprints fade like jokes forgotten,
As waves roll in, the sand gets rotten.
A starfish winks, quite brazenly,
While kids build kingdoms, oh so free!

Sneaky seagulls swipe a fry,
While folks sunbathe, they flap and fly.
A toddler's tantrum, a frisbee's flight,
Mismatched laughter fills the night.

Roll out beach towels, make it grand,
Only to find it's covered in sand.
"Check your pockets," an elder sighs,
"Your snack is gone, to no surprise!"

With goofy grins and sandy toes,
The water's warm, yet sunshine glows.
Under the light, where shadows play,
Memories crafted in a dreamlike ballet.

Enchanted Sands Beneath a Softening Light

With shovels raised, they plot their fate,
Sandcastles rise, but will they wait?
Dramatic waves, a tidal spree,
As jellyfish float like sweet tea.

A kite gets stuck in a seagull's nest,
While beachgoers wear life vests — dressed!
Umbrellas tilt, the wind takes charge,
Crab battles on, they're always at large!

Sandy snacks, each one a delight,
But ants arrive as if to invite.
"Just one bite," a swimmer declares,
As shell-collectors make puzzled stares.

Under this light, where chaos reigns,
And laughter bubbles like summer rains.
From goofy antics to splashes wide,
Every moment is an ocean ride.

Embracing Light in Porcelain Winds

Waves tickle toes, pure joy surrounds,
While laughter mingles with surfy sounds.
A dog runs by with treasures galore,
In a chase with seaweed and more!

Flip-flops forgotten, bare feet sprint,
As three-horned fish swim, brazen hints.
Children parade with pails held high,
Balloons drift away — oh me, oh my!

Coconut hats and sunglasses bright,
A seagull struts, claiming the night.
Sandy sandwiches from yesterday's feast,
A picnic mix-up, to say the least!

In this light, where silliness blooms,
And ocean scents lift all our glooms.
With memories tucked like seaweed strands,
We embrace each laugh, guided by hands.

The Calm Before the Stars

As the sun dips low, we run amok,
Chasing seagulls with our mismatched socks.
Laughter bubbles, waves do cheer,
We're all just kids, let's make that clear.

Buckets in hand, we build our dreams,
A castle that leans, or so it seems.
Sand in our hair, oh what a sight,
Mom says it's cute, but dad's not quite right.

The tide creeps close, we're on our toes,
Urgency mounts as the water flows.
"Quick, grab a shell!" someone will shout,
In the race against waves, we flounder about.

With each splash, we shriek and giggle,
The sun's slow farewell makes us wiggle.
Stars come out, it's time for a cheer,
For every silly moment we hold dear.

A Symphony in Sunsets

Crayon skies burst with colors so loud,
We laugh as our shadows dance with the crowd.
A beach ball bounces into someone's drink,
Who thought beach parties would be such a stink?

The ocean hums a silly tune,
As we all attempt to out-swim the moon.
A crab in a hat joins our funky crew,
Waving its claws as if saying, "Boo!"

Seashells are treasures, or so we decree,
But the best prize is the jellyfish spree.
One squishy touch, and screams fill the air,
We're all just squids with messy hair.

Sandwiches fly, who knew they could soar?
Seagulls make off with our picnic galore.
With a wink and a grin, we shrug and we sway,
Tomorrow's another goofy beach day.

Meditations by Twilight Waters

Footprints in sand, a path of our roam,
We try to decide if we're near or far from home.
With a coconut drink, I sip and I ponder,
Is the ocean approaching? I should really wander.

A pelican lands, acting quite grand,
Faking a dive, causing chaos on land.
We giggle at nature's odd little jest,
As the sunset blushes, we feel truly blessed.

"Do you hear that?" one friend cries with glee,
The sound of waves or just laughter, you see.
As the tide rolls in, our worries take flight,
We'll just blame the gulls for our snack pillow fight.

As twilight falls, we take stock of the fun,
We've collected stories and jokes by the ton.
With a wave to the sea and a laugh at the shore,
We'll be back again, to create even more.

Sunkissed Memories

Sunscreen applied, oh joy, what a mess,
Sticky and slippery, we move with finesse.
Beach towels laid out, but they're a bit damp,
We laugh as we sit in a seaweed camp.

A frisbee flies, aimed straight at my head,
I duck down just in time, or so it is said.
With giggles erupting, sand covers me whole,
Moments like these warm the deepest of souls.

Sea stars and laughter, they scatter like foam,
We gather our treasures to keep and to roam.
Each memory glows like a treasure bright,
While we plot more adventures under the twilight.

As the sun waves goodnight, we wave back with cheer,
For tomorrow we'll gather, our silly crew here.
With sunburns and stories, we'll sit side by side,
In the warmth of our hearts, our joy will abide.

The Sunkissed Horizon

The sun smiles wide upon the sea,
Seagulls dance in a wobbly spree.
A crab in shorts, ready to prance,
As waves invite him to join the dance.

Children giggle, buckets in hand,
Building castles, oh so grand.
One topples over, laughter spills,
As sand flies high in splendid thrills.

Sunscreen thick as cake on noses,
A beach ball bounces, someone dozes.
Bikini tops that slip and slide,
A chase begins, let's take a ride!

As the sun dips down with flair,
My ice cream drips, oh, what a scare!
A flip-flop toss, my drink takes flight,
Tonight we'll talk of this delight!

Traces of Light on Water

Waves like giggles lap the shore,
Sunlight sprinkles, wanting more.
A dog zooms past, a stick in tow,
While sandy toes make footprints slow.

Fishermen argue who's the best,
While one yells, "I caught a jest!"
The fish they claim is tall and stout,
But only minnows poke about.

A lady's hat takes off in flight,
Chasing the breeze, what a sight!
Other hats join in, what a crew,
A party formed, oh, who knew?

With laughter spilling like the tide,
We toss our worries far and wide.
As dusk wraps up the silly chase,
We wave goodbye to the bright face!

A Cadence of Waves and Light

The waves play tag with the sun's glow,
Tickling toes in the foamy flow.
A hermit crab in fancy wear,
Proclaims, "I'm stylish, how do I fare?"

Flip-flops squeak, a rhythmic beat,
As someone snacks on ice-cold treats.
A seagull eyes it with a plea,
"Hey, save some fries, will you for me?"

A parachute of colorful flight,
Whirls overhead, a silly sight.
With squeals and giggles, we take a shot,
Splashing around, giving it all we've got.

The sun yawns wide, day's at its end,
A sandcastle falls, it's time to mend.
With pixie dust in the twilight sway,
We'll dream of the fun until the next day!

The Silken Touch of Evening

Evening rests on the ocean's face,
With soft whispers and a warm embrace.
A jellyfish floats with grace and flair,
While onlookers shout, "Is that a chair?"

Pinch me, it's a sunset dance,
Colors blend in a vivid trance.
A tired pelican on a post,
Seems to ponder what matters most.

Kids dig deep for buried treasure,
While parents snooze in sun's soft leisure.
A pair of flip-flops missed the boat,
Floating away on a sandy moat.

As laughter fades with the light's retreat,
We gather shells, oh, what a treat!
With hearts aglow, we say "Goodnight!"
Tomorrow's mischief is sure to ignite!

The Last Ember of the Day

Seagulls laugh, they steal my fries,
The sun waves bye, in goofy guise.
A crab does the cha-cha on the sand,
While I just hope it won't take my hand.

Umbrellas flip, like sails in flight,
Sandcastles crumble, a silly sight.
Kids run fast, tripping on their feet,
While ice creams melt, a sticky treat.

A dog digs deep, looking for bones,
But finds a flip-flop – it's now well-known.
Waves crash loud, as if to jest,
Nature's humor, we're all quite blessed.

With each wave, a giggle escapes,
From sunburnt noses to tan-lined shapes.
As day bids adieu with a wink and a nudge,
We dance on the sand, and never begrudge.

Echoes of Light's Departure

The sky's a circus, orange and pink,
A seagull swoops down, what do you think?
With popcorn dreams painted on the shore,
Laughing at sandcastles, now folklore.

A flip-flop flies, caught in a breeze,
I chase it down, and yell "Oh please!"
As tide rolls in – oh what a tease,
Slipping and sliding, I fall with ease.

Laughter echoes, a sweet serenade,
As beach towels toss like a juggler's parade.
Suntrapped picnickers munch on their chips,
While toddlers create oceanic slips.

Fire pits crackle, the night takes hold,
But first we chase bubbles, shiny and bold.
In the fading glow, we spin and twirl,
As light bids farewell, in this sandy whirl.

Laughter of the Setting Sun

Wave after wave, we giggle and splash,
Time moves swiftly, oh what a dash!
My toes turned prunes, as I frolic about,
While kids make tidal monsters without a doubt.

A jellyfish drifts, a translucent joke,
Someone yells, "Catch it!" – uh-oh, it's broke!
In this wacky scene of sand and foam,
The sun waves goodbye, yet we feel like home.

Shadows stretch long, but we run in glee,
Building our fort, "It's a fortress!" says he.
Clams flip and flop, with laughter so bright,
As the horizon melts into soft evening light.

With playful breezes tossing our hair,
We chase our dreams in the salty air.
As day sets, we grin, forever young,
In the timeless laughter that's always sung.

Driftwood and Dappled Light

The sun dribbles down like melted ice cream,
While I try to balance on the driftwood beam.
A hermit crab peeks, then hides in a shell,
"Hey buddy, no worries, you fit in so well!"

Boys chase beach balls, but slip on a shell,
While laughter erupts, like a ringing bell.
We sip on our drinks, "Is this coconut?"
Turns out it's soda – now that's what's up!

Even the wind seems to giggle and dance,
As flip-flops fly off, taking their chance.
With painted skies, we twirl about,
In this whimsy world, there's no need to pout.

As the day gently waves its last goodbye,
We gather our treasures and say, "Oh my!"
With driftwood remains and memories bright,
We march home, leaving giggles in the night.

A Tapestry of Dusk

The sun slips down, a lazy tongue,
Telling the sea that it's time to run.
Shadows stretch like a cat so sly,
While seagulls squawk, oh my oh my!

Beach towels flutter like flags of play,
As kids chase waves, then run away.
Sandy crabs with a pinch and a flick,
Dance to the rhythm, a comical trick!

The surf giggles as it rolls and curls,
Tickling toes of all the boys and girls.
Laughter bubbles in the salty air,
With every splash, someone's getting rare!

So grab your shades and a snack with flair,
Life's a circus amidst the salty air.
This tapestry we weave won't fade,
As we laugh and play in this sunset parade.

Horizon's Gleaming Kiss

The horizon grins, a cheeky tease,
With colors that swirl like a big icy breeze.
Flip-flops fly as we skip and hop,
No one quite knows when they'll flop!

Chasing the sunshine with squeals of delight,
Seagulls dive-bombing, oh what a sight!
Sand in our hair, and laughter galore,
Each wave that crashes, we want even more!

The sun's on a break, but it won't be shy,
As it tosses sparkles to dazzle our eye.
We pose like models, then trip on our toes,
With goofy grins, the camera only knows!

So here's to the laughter, the sun's cheeky kiss,
We'll dance through the dusk, what a glorious bliss!
With memories made, we'll treasure this sight,
Long after the "oh no's" and "wow's" delight.

Sand's Warm Glow

Barefoot adventures on warm, soft ground,
Crafting sandcastles, the kings we crowned.
But watch for the waves, they like to tease,
One little splash, drenching with ease!

The sun feels sticky like a melted treat,
As we munch on snacks and kick up our feet.
Seashells are treasures, or so we are told,
Until our pockets weigh like a brick of gold!

Jellyfish float by with a wobbly grace,
Sending us running, oh what a race!
With laughter echoing as we dodge and weave,
Making memories that we'll hardly believe!

And when the twilight dips its brush,
We'll giggle and munch, in playful hush.
For sandy days near the rolling foam,
Are sweet, silly moments that feel like home.

Light Dancing on Water

The sun does a shimmy, a glimmer and twirl,
While fishermen frown over bait that won't swirl.
Children spin like tops, all arms and giggles,
Dropping their ice cream, oh how it dribbles!

Waves waltz on by with a splash and a cheer,
Inviting our toes for a dip, oh dear!
Sandy umbrellas bow to the breeze,
As the crabs join the dance, with moves that tease.

A beach ball's bouncing in bright, silly arcs,
While surfers as mermaids make spectacular sparks.
Oh the folly of mismatched flip-flops galore,
When one goes left, and the other wants more!

As the day wraps up in hues so bright,
We twirl in the sand till the stars peek light.
With laughter that echoes, and hearts full of glee,
This beachside adventure is our jubilee!

www.ingramcontent.com/pod-product-compliance
Lightning Source LLC
Chambersburg PA
CBHW052221090526
44585CB00015BA/1411